# Pasta for Wimps

# Pasta
# for Wimps

**Carlo Lai**

Photography by Matt Cohen

Sterling Publishing Co., Inc.
New York

Created by Penn Publishing Ltd.

Design: Michel Opatowski

Photography: Matt Cohen

Editor: Phyllis Glazer

10 9 8 7 6 5 4 3 2 1

**Library of Congress Cataloging-in-Publication Data**

Lai, Carlo

   Pasta for wimps / Carlo Lai ; photograpy by Matt Cohen.

     p. cm

   Includes index.

   ISBN 1-4027-1008-9

    Cookery (Pasta) I. Title.

TX809.M17L345 2004

641.8'22–dc22                2004051189

Published by Sterling Publishing Co., Inc.

387 Park Avenue South New York, NY 10016

© 2004 by Sterling Publishing Co., Inc.

Distributed in Canada by Sterling Publishing

ᶜ/ₒ Canadian Manda Group, 165 Dufferin Street

Toronto, Ontario, Canada M6K 3H6

Distributed in Great Britain by Chrysalis Books Group PLC

The Chrysalis Building, Bramley Road,

London W10 6SP, England

Distributed in Australia by Capricorn Link (Australia) Pty. Ltd.

P.O. Box 704, Windsor, NSW 2756, Australia

*Printed in China*

*All rights reserved*

Sterling ISBN: 1-4027-1008-9

*To my mother Maria, a wonderful parent and a superb cook, who instilled in me my passion for pasta.*

*To my beloved wife Ziva, for her support and love throughout the years, and to my children Giorgio and Gaia, in the hope that they'll continue our family's culinary traditions with their children.*

# Introduction

My mother took me into the kitchen when I was about three years old and said, "Look, Carlo, today I'm going to make pasta and now that you're a big boy, you're going to help me." I was so proud.

Then she made the dough in a big wooden bowl, gave me a little ball of dough to play with, and fed the rest of it through what looked to me like a metal monster that stomped on it like a cement roller, until the dough came out of the monster's mouth looking like snakes. Together we draped it on the drying rack, and waited for it to dry. This was my first tagliatelle—or fettuccine (the name depends on where in Italy you are from, but more about that later).

It was like **magic**.
**Today, making fresh pasta is still like magic to me.**

Milan, city of *haute couture*.  The place where the living is fast—and the cooking takes time. That's where I was born. But it was in the kitchen that I actually grew up, helping my mother stir the minestrone and stuff the tortellini in our family restaurant. When I was 16, I decided to study cooking formally (in Italy it takes five years!), but despite my warm Italian heart, Milan was simply too cold, and our family decided to move to Sardinia, where the weather is warmer. And there we opened another restaurant, called *El Cervelee de Milan* (The Good Tastes of Milan), where we still make our own bread and fresh pasta every day, and cook great Italian food, with a Sardinian touch.

It was at our restaurant that I first met Frank, an American writer who used to have lunch there every day, always at the same table in the corner, always ordering *ricotta-stuffed spinach ravioli in butter and fresh sage sauce* before his main course. "Frankie," I asked one day, "you love the ravioli so much, why don't you learn to make it yourself when you go home?"

He was astounded. "Make it myself?" he said. "Carlo, *amico mio*. When it comes to fresh pasta, you are a Ferrari, and I'm simply a Fiat 500. A wimp, you see." What is this wimp? I wondered; I had never heard the word before. "A wimp can be intelligent, creative, thoughtful—a wonderful person, like myself; but at the same time, fearful of something strange or new. Someone, also like myself, who believes that for some reason, God has given him two left hands.

There's no hope, Carlo. You'll just have to send the ravioli to me in America."

But I am Italian, and when I decide something, I'm like the Trevi Fountain in Rome—I cannot be moved. I decided I would write a cookbook. It would be an easy book, with easy-to-follow directions and lots of pictures so that even a "wimp" could understand. And I would call it *Pasta for Wimps*—for Frank, his friends, and all of you out there for whom pasta is a passion. That is how this book came to be.

But first, to clarify where I'm coming from, I'd like to tell you a little about the history of the great Italian kitchen, and the real history of pasta:

Although many people consider French cookery to be the **mama of all western cuisines**, it is really the Italian kitchen that holds that claim to fame. It all dates back to the ancient Romans, who found some of their inspiration in both Greece and Asia, and combined that knowledge with ingredients found in their native land. In 1533, when Catherine de' Medici traveled from Florence to France to marry the future King Henry II, she brought her own battery of cooks who taught the French exciting new dishes, including sweets and ices—the origin of the fabulous Italian ices that are enjoyed all over the world today.

**Pasta is also an ancient Italian food, first mentioned in a thirteenth-century cookbook, published five**

years *before* **Marco Polo returned from his famous journey to China.** That means that by the thirtenth century, Italians were already eating many forms of pasta, like vermicelli and a kind of tortellini. So much for the Marco Polo noodle theory! Polo did make an important contribution, however: his writings—and his discoveries—led to the opening up of a direct trade route to the spices of the Far East. In fact, the most glittering palaces of romantic Venice were built with the profits from the spice trade, which until then had been monopolized by Arab middlemen. (And that, incidentally, is how nutmeg got into the Italian kitchen.)

You know, I'm sure, about Michelangelo, da Vinci and other great Italian artists. But did you know that my ancestors were also instrumental in assimilating many products of the New World and introducing them to the rest of Europe? The list includes the tomato; the pimento (red bell pepper), which was originally discovered by the Spanish conquistadors; the potato, imported from Peru in 1530; and corn, the grain we use today to create our beloved polenta.

But above all else, Italians have a passion for pasta. There is no lunch or dinner without it, though in Italy we eat it only as a *primo piatto*—a first course, never a main course as in America. Over the centuries each region has developed its own type of pasta, and sauce to go with it, and sometimes the same dishes will have different names in different regions, which can be very confusing—even for Italians!

In this book, you'll find a guide to the basic utensils and

ingredients that you'll need to make delicious fresh pasta at home, just as I do, my mother does, and her grandmother and ancestors did before her. As you turn the pages, you'll see clear-cut instructions for making spaghetti, fettuccine, ravioli, tortellini, gnocchi and lasagne, and authentic recipes for traditional sauces like Napoletana, Bolognese (Ragu), Aglio e Olio and Pesto.

As each chapter unfolds, there will be other tempting and tantalizing ideas for serving all the great pasta you're going to make—for meat lovers and veggies alike. And all along the way, you'll find the trade secrets that most chefs don't like to share—but I do.

So roll up your sleeves, pour yourself a glass of good Italian wine and join me for a culinary adventure. We're going to create food and fragrances so amazing, you'll feel as if you were eating with me at a table overlooking the blue Mediterranean, savoring the gentle winds in your hair and the sun on your face.

*Buon Appetito!*

*Carlo*

# The Basics

# Tools of the Pasta Master

Making fresh pasta, my friends, doesn't really require any special equipment, except for a food processor to make the dough (although my mother still makes it by hand!) and a pasta machine. And because preparing and cooking pasta and its sauces is so basic and easy, you probably have all the rest of the necessary tools and utensils already on hand. You'll find anything that's missing in any supermarket or department store.

### 1. Cheese Grater and Fresh Nutmeg Grater

There's nothing like the taste of freshly grated Parmesan cheese. The pre-grated commercial varieties are almost always inferior. The same goes for nutmeg!

### 2. Colander

When pasta is done, it must be drained, mixed with sauce and served immediately. The colander begins that process. You can also use it to drain eggplant slices that are salted before cooking, to help remove their bitter juices. Make sure the holes are not too large, especially if you like angel hair pasta or orzo!

### 3. Cutting Board

A wooden board is preferable, and has been proven more hygienic than a plastic board. Use a separate board for cutting raw meat, fish or seafood.

### 4. Heavy Frying Pan

I use a 12" pan with 2-3" sides for preparing four servings of pasta. Increase the size according to the number of servings.

### 5. Kitchen Scale

### 6. Kitchen Towels

### 7. Knives

I use a sharp 8" knife for most pasta projects.

### 8. Lemon Zester

### 9. Pasta Drying Rack

## 10. Pasta Machine

When choosing a pasta machine, remember: bigger is not necessarily better. The small ones work just fine and may be easier to handle. Just make sure that it is made in Italy and includes different heads for fettuccine and ravioli. Electric models are also available, but to me they are like driving a car with an automatic transmission; they may be convenient but I still prefer the control and the feel of a manual machine—even in my restaurant, where I make large quantities of pasta.

a. Head for fettuccine
b. Head for ravioli

## 11. Pasta Pots

Especially made for cooking pasta, these pots are handy, but optional. This version has a tightly fitted cover with drainage holes.

When the pasta is done, you just attach the cover and turn the pot over in the sink. Shake a bit, and you have perfectly drained pasta.

## 12. Rolling Pin

## 13. Sifter

## 14. Stainless Steel Bowls

Easy to clean and attractive, stainless steel bowls are light and unbreakable. It's a good idea to have assorted sizes on hand.

## 15. Wooden Spoons

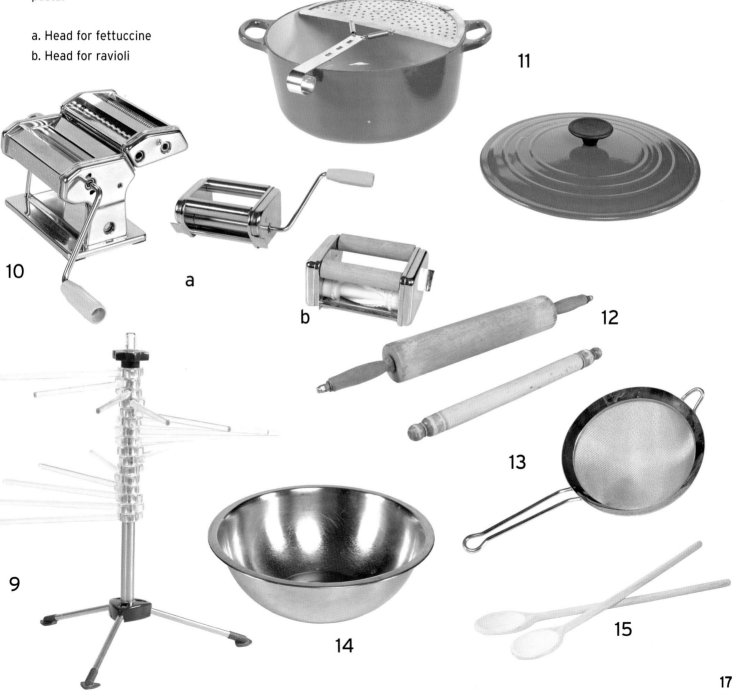

10

a

b

11

12

13

9

14

15

# The Italian Pantry

Although many of the Italian dishes we cook now were first created in the royal courts of the Medicis in Florence, the Sforzas in Milan and the Renaissance Popes, those flavors have long since mingled with the earthier, more humble accents of regional kitchens and evolved into the straightforward yet spirited Italian cuisine we know today.

The basic ingredients are simple and can be found in every supermarket, while the few more unusual ingredients can be found in specialty stores. Make sure to look for the very freshest vegetables, herbs and spices, and for best results avoid ready-made items like prepared salad dressings, pasta sauces, or pre-grated cheese.

*To make fresh pasta you'll need:*

### Durum Semolina

The best pasta in the world is made from durum, a high-protein type of hard wheat that helps the pasta retain its texture when cooked. Semolina, the endosperm of durum, is a granular substance that resembles sugar. The ready-made quality pasta industry uses durum semolina to make macaroni and spaghetti, and durum flour, a by-product of semolina milling, to make noodles. I use durum semolina to make all my pasta.

Both durum semolina and durum flour are sold commercially in some supermarkets and most specialty food stores.

### Eggs

Medium-sized eggs are used in all the recipes in this book. Back home in our restaurant in Sardinia, we prefer to use free-range eggs for the rich color of their yolks.

### Olive Oil

In Italy we use refined olive oil for making pasta dough and for other cooking purposes, and robustly flavored extra-virgin olive oil only for salads.

**Semolina**

**Eggs**

**Plum Tomatoes**

**Olive Oil**

*For sauces and seasoning, you'll need:*

### Butter

Use only unsalted butter.

### Canned Plum Tomatoes

Although my ancient Roman ancestors never knew them, tomatoes are certainly an integral part of modern Italian cooking. In summer, when ripe, fresh tomatoes are in season, use them instead of canned tomatoes. But during the rest of the year, when fresh tomatoes in many countries taste like cotton, I recommend buying rich-flavored Italian-packed whole plum tomatoes.

### Cream

Use sweet cream (heavy cream).

### Mushrooms & Porcini Mushrooms

Italians love mushrooms, but of all mushrooms, porcini, or *Boletus edulis*, are our favorites. Available in all different sizes, fresh porcini have a meaty texture and a full-bodied, earthy flavor that make them suitable for anything from grilling to pasta sauces and salads. When I was little, we used to collect them in the mountains outside Milan in fall. Today you can find them in most specialty stores in America, where they are unfortunately quite pricey. Portobello mushrooms can be substituted, but they lack the rich flavor of porcini. Dried porcini can also be substituted.

When choosing fresh porcini, look for ones that are firm-textured, with no blemishes or brown spots. Never wash them before storing, since they will spoil very quickly. Instead, you can store them unwashed in a paper bag at the bottom of your refrigerator for up to three days. Although many aficionados claim that mushrooms should only be wiped with a damp cloth just before using, I like to wash them quickly so they do not absorb too much water. Never let them soak!

### Pine Nuts

Also known as pignolia. Available in supermarkets and specialty stores.

### Red & White Wines

For a premium sauce, you'll need a premium wine. Never cook with any wine you wouldn't drink! I always cook with dry wines.

### Thyme

Thyme has a subtle aroma and a slightly minty flavor that we like to use sparingly in the Italian kitchen. It's an herb that not only tastes good, but is also believed to help improve digestion.

### Tartufo Bianco (White Truffle)

In the northern Italian province of Piemonte, the incomparable white truffle, *il tartufo bianco d'Alba*, grows wild beneath the surface of the soil. The grayish-amber fungus is sniffed out by truffle hounds that are specially trained for this purpose. Found in specialty stores and quite expensive, even a tiny bit adds an incredible aroma and flavor to pasta dishes.

Thyme

Porcini

## DRIED PORCINI MUSHROOMS

Can't find fresh porcini? No problem: Dried porcini also add superb flavor and aroma to sauces and soups, and are available almost everywhere. Look for sliced porcini that are light-colored—mainly cream or beige. Packages with crumbly bits are inferior. To rehydrate them before using, soak in a bowl of warm water for around 20 to 30 minutes. Strain and save the flavorful liquid and add it to soups and sauces. Rinse the reconstituted porcini in many changes of water to remove any embedded grit. Store dried porcini in an airtight bag in the refrigerator or freezer.

# Italian Cheeses

Parmigiano. Ricotta. Gorgonzola. Ahhh. Where would we Italians be without our beloved cheeses? We buy them like treasures at the *mercatino* (market), where they are lovingly displayed in all their glory, and bring them home to use on pasta, pizza and almost everything we make. Here are some of my favorites, and the ones that (not coincidentally) we'll be using in this book. Look for them in Italian markets, cheese shops and some supermarkets.

### Gorgonzola (also known as Stracchino di Gorgonzola)

Gorgonzola comes from Lombardy, the region around Milan, my birthplace. Centrally located, it was a stopping place for "tired" (*stracca*) cattle and their herdsmen during their long spring and fall treks to and from seasonal pastures. Thus, twice a year, the area was so overflowing with milk, the natives used it to make cheese!

Although you'll find both sweet (*dolce*) and sharp, aged Gorgonzola (*naturale*) in most shops, in our recipes we'll be using just dolce.

### Italian Gruviera

This is the Italian version of Swiss Gruyère cheese, an unpasteurized cow's milk cheese with a brown, pebbled rind and a smooth, creamy-beige interior. If you can't find Gruviera, substitute Emmental.

### Mozzarella

Back in the old days, mozzarella cheese was made from water buffalo's milk. Today it is made from cow's milk. My mother always taught us to use whole-milk mozzarella because of its creamy texture and delicate flavor, but part skim cheese can be used if desired. (I do not recommend the nonfat form.) This style of mozzarella is best used for cooking and is popular for pizza because of its excellent melting qualities.

But there's also fresh mozzarella, which is usually packaged in whey or water. Generally made from whole milk, it has a much softer texture and a sweet, delicate flavor. *Mozzarella di bufala* (also called buffalo mozzarella), made with water-buffalo milk, is considered the finest, but most buffalo mozzarella available in America is blended with cow's milk. If you're fortunate enough to have an Italian grocery in your neighborhood, you might also find bocconcini, 1" diameter balls often sold marinated in olive oil, and a smoked version called *mozzarella affumicata*. They're both great on bread with salt, pepper, and a little olive oil, or in salads.

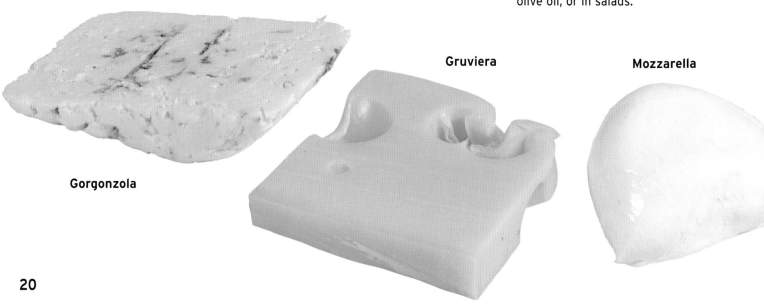

**Gorgonzola**

**Gruviera**

**Mozzarella**

### Parmesan

Believe it or not, in my entire life as a cook, I never spent a day without *Parmigiano-Reggiano*—the genuine Parmesan cheese. Manufactured in a centuries-old traditional method that allows no additives and no substances other than milk and rennet, it is produced in Emilia-Romagna, a region of Italy whose boundaries are fixed in Italian law. Real Parmigiano-Reggiano requires at least 12 months of ripening, meticulously monitored by master cheesemakers. There's nothing like it.

Want to impress your family and dazzle your friends? Use the real McCoy. Sorry—those pre-grated Parmesan cheeses sold in supermarkets lack the character and taste of the real thing. Use them only if you're desperate.

Parmigiano-Reggiano will keep for a long time in the refrigerator, so if you buy a large piece, cut it into wedges with some rind still attached to each wedge. Wrap them separately with two or three layers of foil and check occasionally. If you notice them drying out, wrap in damp cheesecloth, cover with foil and refrigerate overnight. The next day, remove the foil, discard the cheesecloth, wipe dry with a paper towel, and then rewrap it in foil and return it to the refrigerator.

### Pecorino Romano

Pecorino Romano, usually called just Romano, is a sheep's milk cheese whose name is derived from *pecora*, the Italian word for sheep. An aged cheese with a distinctive sharp flavor and texture (it crumbles and flakes easily), it might be called the southern Italian answer to Parmigiano-Reggiano as a favorite for grating over pasta. The best Romano is made in the province of Rome, where the cheese originated, though today much of it comes from Sardinia, home of the largest sheep population in Italy.

To store it, wrap this cheese in heavy paper and keep it in the bottom of the refrigerator. Unaged, it will keep for two to four weeks. Well-aged, it will keep indefinitely.

### Pecorino Sardo

Known as *Pecorino Sardo, Fiore Sardo,* or simply *Sardo*, this cheese comes from the island of Sardinia, where we have our restaurant. Made from whole milk produced by free-ranging sheep that graze on fragrant Mediterranean shrubs, it is a gently piquant, firm sheep's milk cheese with a more delicate taste than Pecorino Romano. Look for a brown- to buff-colored rind and a smooth interior with no holes or cracks. Though it is hard to find in America, *Mamma mia*—is it good!

### Ricotta

Unlike most of our cheeses that have been made for hundreds of years, ricotta cheese is only about 100 years old. Invented in Rome using the whey that remained after the production of Romano cheese, ricotta was created by enterprising cheesemakers who discovered that disposing of whey in sewers and rivers killed the fish. Instead, they turned it into a low-fat, protein-rich, fresh cheese—an Italian take on cottage cheese.

In Italy, we make ricotta cheese from sheep's milk or the milk of cows, goats or water buffalo. American ricotta is sweeter and moister than Italian ricotta, but all types can be used in my pasta dishes or eaten as is.

**Ricotta**

**Parmesan**

**Pecorino Romano**

**Pecorino Sardo**

# Meats & Seafood

### Bacon (Pancetta)

In Italy we use bacon not only as a food, but also as a flavoring, especially in sauces like Carbonara (page 48) or all'Amatriciana (page 58). Choose bacon with at least 30% fat, and drain off some of the fat if preferred.

### Ground Lean Meat

Buy freshly ground, lean meat if possible. Ask your butcher for meat with 10% fat or less.

### Lean Pork

With 10% fat or less.

### Mortadella

A type of bologna manufactured in Bologna since medieval times, when tradition holds that it was ground in a mortar. Bologna is still the largest sausage-producing region in Italy.

### Parma Ham (Prosciutto)

Cured in the mountain air, Parma ham is world famous. One taste and you'll know why.

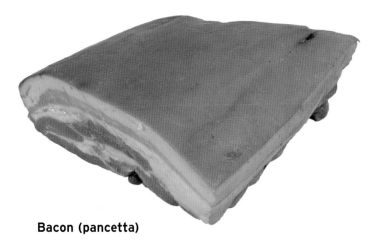

Bacon (pancetta)

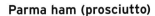

Parma ham (prosciutto)

Ground lean meat

Lean pork

### Anchovies (flat)

In this book we'll be using oil-packed anchovies, rather than salt-packed ones.

### Calamari

Remember to rinse the calamari very well inside and remove any cartilage. Always cook briefly or it will turn rubbery.

### Octopus

I always recommend buying small octopuses. The smaller they are, the more tender the meat is after cooking.

### Shrimp

I prefer to use medium-sized shrimp for pasta dishes.

### Mussels

Always buy fresh mussels that are tightly closed, and discard any that do not open after cooking.

**Anchovies (flat)**

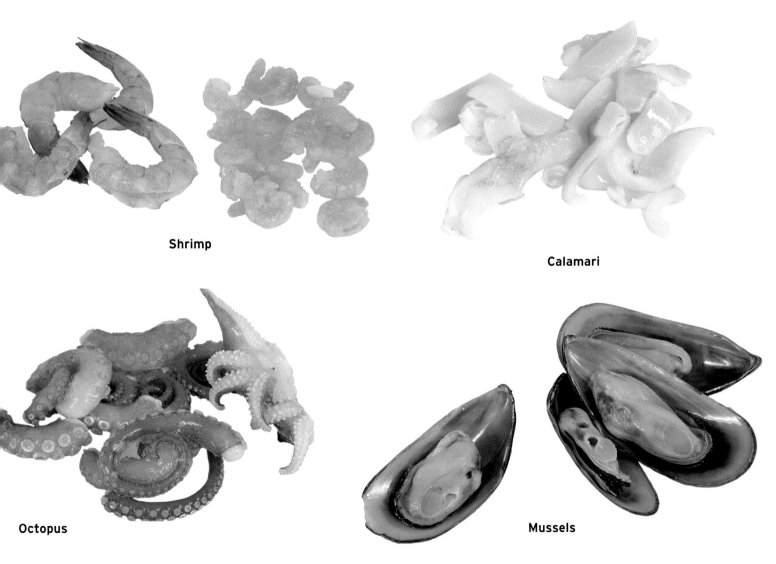

**Shrimp**

**Calamari**

**Octopus**

**Mussels**

# Herbs & Spices

Like the different parts of America, each region of Italy has its own history, its own special produce, and its own distinctive way of preparing food. We Italians may not agree about soccer teams, politics or women—but when it comes to the kitchen, if we don't have parsley, we'd rather eat out. In fact, in Italian, when you keep running into someone, you say that the person is "like parsley—found in every sauce!"

Wherever we come from, Italians all use fresh parsley, sage, rosemary and...basil. Never cilantro. Take them home lovingly, rinse in several changes of cold water, let dry and wrap in a slightly damp paper towel. Place, towel and all, in a resealable bag and store in the refrigerator. Most will keep for several days.

Since I know most of you will probably end up with more fresh herbs than you know what to do with, why not make seasoning cubes out of the leftovers? Process them separately or together in a food processor with enough olive oil to make a paste, and freeze in small ice cube trays. Once frozen, the cubes can be stored in a plastic bag or plastic container in the freezer, and added to tomato sauce, pasta dishes and soups. You can even defrost them and dilute them with a little extra olive oil to drizzle over prepared foods.

When it comes to Italian herbs and spices, here are the major players:

## Basil

I can't imagine Italian cooking without basil, whose name comes from the Greek word *basileus*, meaning "king." Actually, the herb originated in India and was brought to Italy by way of the spice route thousands of years ago. We use it with pasta, salads, cheeses and in all kinds of sauces. To retain basil's bright color, be careful not to bruise the leaves while rinsing or storing, and slice, rather than chop, them.

## Chili Pepper (not powder) or Flakes

Just one or two will do the trick. Remove the ribs and seeds if preferred.

## Garlic

Always use fresh garlic—never dried powder or flakes. It's indispensable in Italian cooking, and proven healthy, too. If you don't use it often (although you should), store the peeled cloves covered in olive oil in the refrigerator. You can season pasta with the oil as well. After dinner, you can eliminate "garlic breath" by chewing fresh parsley as a natural mouth freshener.

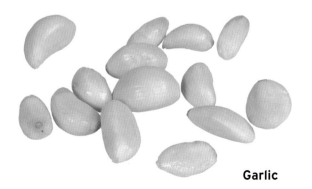

**Garlic**

### Nutmeg

Just a pinch will do it. Buy a little nutmeg grater, and freshly grate your own.

### Oregano

Oregano comes from the same family as mint, and is a cousin to basil and marjoram. Ours is mild compared to Greek, Spanish and Mexican oregano. If you've only used it on pizza, try it in tomato sauce, pasta sauces, pesto, and with dishes containing eggplant, zucchini, broccoli or onions.

### Parsley

My mother says, "When you have garlic, olive oil and parsley on hand, you can begin to cook." She's right. The flavor combination is a classic in many Italian dishes. We use only flat-leafed ("Italian") parsley, and you'll notice that like a true Italian, I use it to garnish most of my pasta dishes.

### Rosemary

If you seem to be forgetful lately, try some rosemary tea. For centuries, rosemary has been used both in the kitchen and for its herbal benefits. It's thought to help clear the mind, improve memory and aid digestion—all good reasons to use it as Italians do—in sauces and marinades for dishes containing fatty meats, chicken, pork and lamb. Use it fresh or dried, but always sparingly—it's especially pungent.

**IDEA:** Decorate your kitchen with any leftover fresh rosemary sprigs: Tie the stems together with ribbon or twine, and hang upside down in a place with good air circulation. When it dries, store in jars with tightly fitted lids, away from sunlight.

### Sage

Sage is an amazing herb. It not only adds a pungent flavor to pasta, meats and poultry, but its Latin name comes from the word *salvere*, which means "to cure." For thousands of years, sage has been used throughout the Mediterranean to relieve stomach aches, aid digestion, soothe coughs and colds—and chase away the Evil Eye. My dear American friend Frank, who was the inspiration for this book, told me that Native Americans use it as well—in a ceremony to chase away the Evil Spirits.

I use sage to flavor butter sauces for ravioli and other stuffed pastas, or sauté the individual leaves in butter till crisp.

**TIP:** To dry any leftover sage quickly for storage, lay the leaves on clean paper towels and place in the microwave. Cook on high for four minutes. Cool and store in an airtight container.

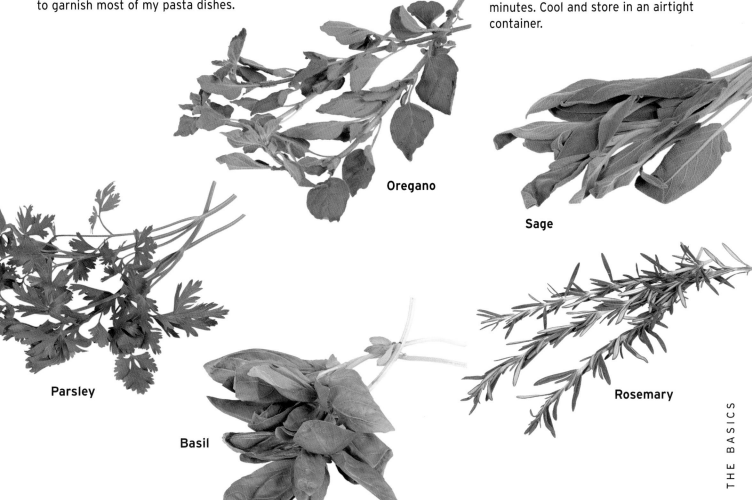

Oregano

Sage

Parsley

Basil

Rosemary

Basic

# Pasta Dough

# Basic Pasta Dough

This is it—the basic dough you can use to make 8 main-course servings of fettuccine, ravioli or tortellini. (Of course, in Italy, where pasta is only served as a first course, this recipe would feed 16!)

Although my mother always makes pasta dough by hand, I opt for the modern approach and use a food processor. It's much easier and quicker, and if you use this generations-old pasta recipe, guaranteed *bellissimo!*

Once you make the dough, follow the instructions in each chapter to turn it into your favorite pasta shape. You can always freeze any unused fresh pasta, preferably in single layers.

**Ingredients:**

2 pounds durum semolina

7 medium eggs, at room temperature

3 tablespoons olive oil

**Serves 8**

*1* Sift the flour into a bowl.

*2* In a medium bowl, beat the eggs together briskly with a wire whisk or fork.

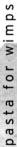

Put the semolina, beaten eggs and olive oil into the bowl of the food processor.

Beginning at medium speed, mix all the ingredients until the mixture forms a ball around the blade.

Remove from the processor and place on a lightly floured work surface. Sprinkle a little flour on top.

**6** Cover with a cloth towel and let rest for 10 minutes.

**7** Divide the dough into 5 equal portions. Knead $^{1}/_{5}$ of the dough at a time for a minute or two until no longer sticky, adding a little more flour if necessary.

**8** Using a lightly floured rolling pin, shape the dough into a 9" x 4" oblong, no more than $^{1}/_{2}$" thick.

**9** Cover the oblong with a kitchen towel and repeat the process, using $^{1}/_{5}$ of the dough each time. Cover each oblong before working on the next.

**10** Now we shape the dough in the machine, starting with the large roller. Position the machine on setting number 1 and use one hand to feed the dough between the rollers (while you crank the handle with the other hand), until it comes out the other side. (The dough will still be thick.)

Change the number to 3 and feed the dough in again. *11*

Change the number to 5 (the thinnest setting), and feed the dough in slowly once more. *12*

Now you are ready to make any of the pastas in this book. Follow the directions in each chapter.

# Garlic & Chili Pepper Pasta Dough

This hot and garlicky combination is great for people who like a little zing! in their pasta. I like it best for spaghetti and fettuccine, especially with Aglio e Olio sauce (page 47), but it also tastes mighty fine as ricotta-stuffed ravioli (page 90).

**Ingredients:**

8 large cloves garlic

2 medium dried chili peppers

2 pounds durum semolina

7 eggs

1 1/2 tablespoons olive oil

**Serves 8**

*1* Place the garlic and chili peppers in the bowl of a food processor, and process to form a paste.

*2* Sift the flour into a bowl.

*3* In a medium bowl, beat the eggs together briskly with a wire whisk or fork.

*4* Put the semolina, beaten eggs and olive oil in the bowl of the food processor.

*5* Beginning at medium speed, mix all the ingredients until the mixture forms a ball around the blade.

*6* Follow steps 5 to 12 of the instructions for basic pasta dough on pages 29–31.

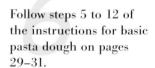

# Italian Herb Pasta Dough

Elegant and flavorful, herb pasta adds a festive touch to any meal. This recipe is perfect for any pasta—from spaghetti to lasagne. Especially good with Napoletana sauce (page 40).

**Ingredients:**

1/2 cup packed fresh basil leaves
1/2 cup packed fresh oregano leaves
1/4 cup fresh thyme leaves
8 tablespoons olive oil
2 pounds durum semolina
6 eggs

**Serves 8**

1 Rinse the herbs in several changes of water, and let dry thoroughly on a kitchen towel. Remove stems and measure the required amount.

2 Place the fresh herbs and olive oil in the bowl of a food processor, and process to a creamy consistency.

3 Sift the flour into a bowl.

4 In a medium bowl, beat the eggs together briskly with a wire whisk or fork.

5 Put the semolina and beaten eggs in the bowl of the food processor.

6 Beginning at medium speed, mix all the ingredients until the mixture forms a ball around the blade.

7 Follow steps 5 to 12 of the instructions for basic pasta dough on pages 29–31.

## PASTA TRICOLORE

Making pasta in three different colors may seem like an awesome task, but it can be quite easy if you prepare each color on a separate day, and freeze it in the shape you want. For "white" pasta (which is really yellow-tinged because of the eggs), use the basic dough recipe on page 28. For green and red pastas, follow the instructions below. Each color serves 8, but you can make half the amount if preferred.

# Green (Spinach) Pasta Dough

**Ingredients:**

8 ounces thawed frozen chopped
    spinach (weight after draining)

6 medium eggs

2 pounds durum semolina

3 tablespoons olive oil

**Serves 8**

*1* Thaw the spinach in a colander, and squeeze out any excess moisture.

*2* Sift the flour into a bowl.

*3* In a medium bowl, beat the eggs together briskly with a wire whisk or fork.

*4* Put the semolina, olive oil, beaten eggs and spinach in the bowl of the food processor.

*5* Beginning at medium speed, mix all the ingredients until the mixture forms a ball around the blade.

*6* Follow steps 5 to 12 of the instructions for basic pasta dough on pages 29–31.

# Red (Tomato) Pasta Dough

**Ingredients:**

2 pounds durum semolina

6 eggs

4 tablespoons olive oil

4 tablespoons Napoletana tomato
   sauce (page 40)

**Serves 8**

1 Sift the flour into a bowl.

2 In a medium bowl, beat the eggs together briskly with a wire whisk or fork.

3 Put the semolina, olive oil, beaten eggs and tomato sauce in the bowl of the food processor.

4 Beginning at medium speed, mix all the ingredients until the mixture forms a ball around the blade.

5 Follow steps 5 to 12 of the instructions for basic pasta dough on pages 28–31.

# Basic Sauces

# Bolognese Sauce

Here's the recipe for classic Bolognese sauce, beloved by people around the world. It originated in Bologna, where it is called *Ragu*!

Use this sauce for pasta or lasagne, or thickened as a stuffing for cannelloni or ravioli. Don't worry about the quantity—you can freeze it for up to six months. The recipe can also be made with the addition of 2 ounces of ground lamb, or using only beef if you like.

**Ingredients:**

1 1/2 pounds lean ground beef (with less than 10% fat)

6-8 ounces lean ground pork

1 large (1/2 pound) onion

1 medium carrot

3 ribs celery

1 large can (1 pound 10 1/2 ounces) peeled plum tomatoes

1 cup olive oil

2 cups dry red wine

5 bay leaves

3 1/2 ounces tomato paste

**Serves 10 or more**

1 Mix the ground beef and pork together in a bowl, using your fingers.

2 Chop the carrot and onion finely. Remove the strings from the celery and chop finely.

3 Place the tomatoes with their juice in a blender or food processor and blend.

4 Heat the olive oil in a large pot. Sauté onion, carrots and celery on low heat, stirring occasionally, for 10 minutes.

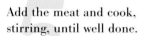 Add the meat and cook, stirring, until well done.

6 Add the red wine and bay leaves, and cook over medium-high heat until reduced by half.

7 Add the tomatoes and let cook, uncovered, for 30 minutes.

8 Add the tomato paste, and salt and pepper to taste. Cook until the sauce is slightly thick and has a deep red color.

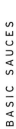

# Napoletana Sauce

Napoletana, from the city of Naples, is the *numero uno* favorite Italian sauce. Real Napoletana is light, and perfect as a base for all recipes calling for tomato sauce. Winter, summer, spring or fall—we always make a big pot of Napoletana and use it throughout the year, for pasta and pizza and as an added flavoring in all kinds of sauces.

This recipe makes 3 quarts (the tomatoes cook down), which is a large amount, I know, but is definitely worth making and freezing. To freeze, cool the sauce and pack in plastic containers until almost full. (If you leave too much air space, ice crystals will develop.) I like to use 1-pound storage containers, so when I defrost the sauce I have enough in each container to serve four.

**Ingredients:**

6 pounds canned peeled plum
   tomatoes (3 1/2  28-ounce cans)

1 large (1/2 pound) onion

1 large carrot

1 cup olive oil

1 tablespoon salt

1/2 tablespoon sugar

Black pepper to taste

Medium basil leaves

**Makes 3 quarts**

**1** Pour the tomatoes and their juice into a blender, and process until completely smooth.

**2** Chop onion and carrot.

Heat the olive oil in a large heavy pot placed over low heat. (It is very important to keep heat low, because tomato sauce burns easily.) Sauté onion and carrot about 5 minutes.

Add the tomatoes and let cook on low heat for 1¹/2 hours, stirring often with a wooden spoon.

When the sauce is done, season with salt, pepper and sugar.

Garnish with basil.

**CARLO'S TIP**
To check if your Napoletana is ready, try my foolproof tip: Put a couple of tablespoons of sauce on a plate and tilt the plate to see if water separates out from the sauce. If you can see water, it isn't ready yet.

# Béchamel Sauce

Béchamel sauce, called *besciamella* in Italian, is one of our most important working sauces. Made correctly, it will give your lasagne a smoother and more delicate texture and taste, and it can be used for all sauces that contain cream—just a little bit (2 tablespoons) will do wonders for the texture.

This is my mother's recipe, and I love it. Always make it fresh—it doesn't take well to freezing.

**Ingredients:**
1/4 cup butter
Salt
Pepper
Nutmeg
1/4 cup flour
2 cups milk

**Makes 2 cups, enough for 4 servings of lasagne**

*1* Melt the butter in a small skillet and add a pinch each of salt, pepper and nutmeg.

*2* Remove from heat and stir in the flour until it is dissolved and the mixture is smooth.

*3* Gradually add the milk, stirring constantly to avoid lumps.

*4* Return to the heat and stir constantly for 10 minutes until the Béchamel thickens.

# Genovese Pesto Sauce

Our beloved pesto sauce originated in the city of Genoa, in the Liguria region, where the weather is much nicer and warmer than anywhere else in the north of Italy. Only about 95 miles separate Milan and Genoa, and yet the weather in the two cities is totally different. Just 60 miles from Milan, there's a tunnel that goes through a mountain. On the Milan side the weather can be cold and rainy, while on the Genovese side it can be warm and sunny at the exact same time. Genoa also boasts retirement communities like those in Miami, and fresh basil grows there all year round.

In Genoa, pesto is always served with a special kind of curled fettuccine called trenette. You can also spread it on bread and sandwiches, use it as a stuffing for mushrooms (top with a little cheese and place in a hot oven until the cheese is melted), or put it on roasted meats or poultry as a flavoring rub.

Pesto can keep for up to two months in the refrigerator, but only if it is covered with a thin layer of olive oil.

**Ingredients:**
5 medium cloves garlic
1/3 cup pine nuts
1 1/4 cups olive oil
2 cups packed basil leaves
1/4 cup Parmesan cheese
1/2 cup Pecorino Romano cheese

**Serves 10**

1. Put the garlic and pine nuts in a food processor with a little bit of the olive oil.

2. Process until it looks like a coarse paste.

3. Open the processor and add the basil. Close the top and gradually add a little more oil through the feed tube while the machine is running. Process until the basil is pulverized.

4. Keep the machine running, and add the cheeses and the rest of the oil through the feed tube. Process until a paste is formed.

**CARLO'S TIP**
Use leftover herbs to make different kinds of pesto, or mix different herbs for exciting new pesto combinations.

# Spaghetti

& Spaghettini

# How to Make Fresh Spaghetti or Spaghettini

Everybody loves spaghetti and its little brothers, spaghettini and angel hair pasta.

To make fresh spaghetti, follow the directions for basic pasta dough (page 28), or one of the special pasta variations. Then:

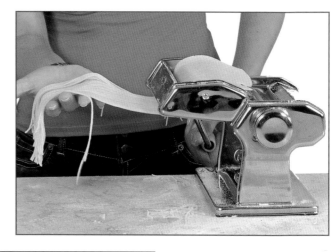

**1** Place the special spaghetti or spaghettini head on the machine.

**2** Cut each oblong leaf of rolled dough into a 12" long piece and feed through the machine. Handle it gently as it comes through the machine. Repeat with the rest of the dough.

**3** Cover a kitchen counter or table with an old white tablecloth or sheet. Spread the already-made spaghetti evenly over the surface and let stand 5 minutes while you work on the next leaf of dough (or spread it on a drying rack). Cover until ready to use. Handle the already-made noodles carefully.

**4** If not using the pasta immediately, dust the bottom of a plastic container with a little flour or cornmeal, fold the spaghetti and place it in one layer in the container. Lay a piece of wax paper or parchment paper on top, cover and freeze.

NOTE: Cook fresh spaghetti for 2$\frac{1}{2}$ minutes, or spaghettini for 1$\frac{1}{2}$ minutes. Drain well.

Next, choose one of the following easy and fabulous sauces—perfect for serving with spaghetti or spaghettini.

# Spaghetti Aglio e Olio
## Spaghetti with Garlic and Olive Oil Sauce

When a group of friends in Italy get the munchies just around midnight, we don't order pizza. Spaghetti Aglio e Olio is our favorite late-night snack. This is my own special version.

In a large pot, bring 3 quarts of water to a boil with 3 tablespoons salt. Now prepare the sauce.

**Ingredients:**

1/4 cup olive oil

3-4 garlic cloves, each sliced lengthwise into 4 pieces

2 chili peppers, or more to taste

2 anchovies

1/4 cup dry white wine

Salt to taste

1/2 cup minced parsley

Spaghetti made from 1/2 basic dough recipe (page 28), or 1 pound dried spaghetti (for a main course)

Extra-virgin olive oil for seasoning

**Serves 4**

1 In a large skillet, heat the olive oil over medium heat. Add the sliced garlic, peppers and anchovies. Use a wooden spoon to stir the mixture, pressing occasionally with the back of the spoon, until the anchovies are broken up and blended into the olive oil. (The oil must not be too hot, or it will fry the anchovies instead of allowing them to "melt" into the olive oil.)

2 Remove the skillet from the heat, and add the wine, a good pinch of salt and half of the parsley. Mix well.

3 Cook fresh spaghetti for 2 1/2 minutes, or spaghettini for 1 1/2 minutes, or dried spaghetti according to package directions. Drain well and add to the skillet. Stir until the strands are coated with sauce.

4 Season with a little extra-virgin olive oil, garnish with the remaining parsley and serve.

# Spaghetti Carbonara
## Spaghetti with Bacon and Cream Sauce

This is one of the most popular sauces for serving with spaghetti.

In a large pot, bring 3 quarts of water to a boil with 3 tablespoons salt. Now prepare the sauce.

**Ingredients:**

10 1/2 ounces bacon (in one piece)

4 egg yolks

1 cup sweet cream

Salt

Black pepper to taste

3 tablespoons unsalted butter, at room temperature

Spaghetti made from 1/2 basic dough recipe (page 28), or 1 pound dried spaghetti (for a main course)

Extra-virgin olive oil for seasoning

1 tablespoon chopped parsley, to garnish

**Serves 4**

*1* Cut the bacon into 1/4" cubes.

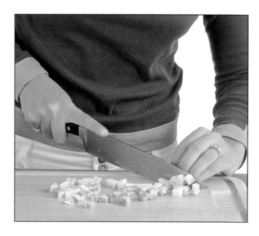

*2* Whisk the eggs, cream, salt and black pepper together in a bowl. Add the room-temperature butter a little at a time until well blended. (If there are any lumps, don't worry, they will melt into the hot pasta.)

*3* Heat a large skillet over medium heat, add the bacon cubes and sauté until crisp. Remove with a slotted spoon and set aside. Drain off most of the fat in the skillet, leaving just a little to flavor the sauce.

*4* Cook fresh spaghetti for 2 ¹/₂ minutes, or spaghettini for 1 ¹/₂ minutes, or dried spaghetti according to package directions. Drain well, reserving 1 tablespoon cooking liquid.

*5* Reheat the bacon over high heat, and add the reserved tablespoon of cooking water.

*6* Transfer the spaghetti to the skillet, season with a little extra-virgin olive oil and mix with a wooden spoon. Add the egg and cream mixture and cook, stirring constantly, for ¹/₂ minute.

*7* Serve immediately, garnished with parsley.

# Spaghetti alle Zucchine
## Spaghetti with Fresh Zucchini Sauce

This light sauce has the scent of summer, with a pronounced garlic flavor. I always cook garlic on low or medium heat, which makes it turn more evenly golden and gives it just a hint of sweetness.

In a large pot, bring 3 quarts of water to a boil with 3 tablespoons salt. Now prepare the sauce.

**Ingredients:**

2 medium zucchini (about 1 pound)

3 tablespoons olive oil

4 cloves garlic, each cut lengthwise into 4 slices

1 medium dried chili pepper, broken into 3 pieces, or ground chili pepper

Spaghetti made from 1/2 basic dough recipe (page 28), or 1 pound dried spaghetti

1/2 cup fresh basil, cut into strips

**Serves 4**

1 Remove a slice from both ends of the zucchini, and slice into 1/4" slices. Slice these into 1/4" julienne. Set aside.

2 Heat the olive oil in a large skillet over medium heat and sauté the garlic until golden (about 2 minutes), stirring occasionally. Add the chili pepper pieces and sauté for 1/2 minute.

**5** Place the cooked pasta in the skillet and heat, stirring, until it is heated through and the sauce covers the strands.

**6** Garnish with basil and serve.

**3** Add the zucchini and sauté on both sides until golden. Lower heat and continue to cook, stirring occasionally, until the zucchini is tender. If the zucchini becomes too dry, add a tablespoon or two of the pasta cooking water or dry white wine. Immediately remove pan from the heat when the zucchini is done.

**4** While the zucchini is cooking, drop fresh spaghetti into the pasta pot and cook for 2¹/₂ minutes, or 1¹/₂ minutes for spaghettini, or according to package directions. Drain well.

# Spaghetti ai Funghi

## Spaghetti with Mushroom Sauce

This sauce is traditionally served in the wintertime with a glass of good wine, such as Barolo. For great flavor and effect, use an assortment of wild mushrooms, available in specialty stores and supermarkets. When you're ready to use them, wipe the mushrooms with a damp paper towel to clean. Peel any discolored pieces off the tops.
I do not recommend rinsing wild mushrooms, since they tend to absorb too much water for this dish.
Always use fresh oregano. Dried oregano just won't do.

In a large pot, bring 3 quarts of water to a boil with 3 tablespoons salt. Now prepare the sauce.

**Ingredients:**

2 tablespoons of olive oil

4 garlic cloves, each cut lengthwise into 4 slices

10 1/2 ounces assorted fresh mushrooms (mixed wild mushrooms, or button mushrooms), coarsely chopped

1/2 cup dry red wine

Spaghetti made from 1/2 basic dough recipe (page 28), or 1 pound dried spaghetti

Salt

Pepper

1/4 cup fresh oregano, finely chopped

**Serves 4**

*1* Heat the olive oil in a large skillet and sauté the garlic over medium heat.
Add the mushrooms and cook for 4 minutes, stirring occasionally.

*2* Add the wine and continue cooking over medium heat until liquid is reduced by half.

*3* Cook fresh spaghetti for 2 1/2 minutes, or 1 1/2 minutes for spaghettini, or according to package directions. Drain well. Add the pasta to the sauce and heat through, stirring.

*4* Season with salt and pepper, garnish with oregano and serve.

pasta for wimps

52

# Spaghetti al Limone
## Spaghetti with Lemon Sauce

Fresh, light and refreshing to the palate.

In a large pot, bring 3 quarts of water to a boil with 3 tablespoons salt. Now prepare the sauce.

**Ingredients:**

1 large lemon

2 1/2 tablespoons butter

1 medium onion, minced

8 ounces prosciutto, cut in 1/2" thick slices, and then into cubes

1 cup sweet cream

Salt

Black pepper

Spaghetti made from 1/2 basic dough recipe (page 28), or 1 pound dried spaghetti

Parsley for garnish

**Serves 4**

1. Julienne the lemon rind into long, thin strips with a zester. Juice half of the lemon.

2. In a large skillet, melt the butter over medium heat and add the minced onion. Stir with a wooden spoon until lightly golden.

3. Add prosciutto cubes and sauté for 2 minutes.

4. Add the lemon juice and cream and cook on medium-high heat until liquid is reduced to half. Season the sauce with salt and pepper.

5. In the meantime, cook fresh spaghetti for 2 1/2 minutes, or 1 1/2 minutes for spaghettini, or according to package directions. Drain well, add to the sauce and heat through, stirring. Garnish with parsley.

# Fettuccine

# How to Make Fresh Fettuccine

We Italians are an interesting lot. We all eat pasta, but sometimes we have different names for the same thing, depending on where we come from. Take fettuccine, for example. In northern Italy, we call it tagliatelle, and from Rome southward–fettuccine. So if I were to go into a restaurant in Rome and order tagliatelle, they'd say to me, "No, not tagliatelle, it's fettuccine"–and probably jack up the price!

Fettuccine is a traditional Roman pasta, but today it is well known all over the world. This pasta can be dressed with a lot of different kinds of sauces based on meat, vegetables, cheese or seafood. To make fresh fettuccine, follow the directions for basic pasta dough (page 28) or one of the special pasta variations.

**1** To make fettuccine, place the fettuccine head on the machine.

**2** Cut each leaf of dough into a 12" long piece and feed through the machine. Handle the fettuccine noodles gently as they come through the machine.

**3** Cover a kitchen counter or table with an old white tablecloth or sheet. Spread the freshly made fettuccine evenly over the surface and let stand 5 minutes while you work on the next leaf of dough (or spread on a drying rack). Cover until ready to use.

**4** If not using the pasta immediately, dust the bottom of a plastic container with a little flour or cornmeal, fold the fettuccine into 8 separate portions and place it in the container in one layer. Lay a piece of waxed paper or parchment paper on top, cover and freeze.

# Fettuccine al Ragu
## Fettuccine with Bolognese Sauce

In a large pot, bring 3 quarts of water to a boil with 3 tablespoons salt. Now prepare the sauce.

**1** Heat the Bolognese sauce in a large skillet.

**2** Drop the fettuccine into the pot and cook for 4 minutes for fresh pasta or according to package directions for dried pasta. Drain.

**3** Transfer the fettuccine to the skillet and mix gently until well coated.

**Ingredients:**

2 cups Bolognese sauce (page 38)

Fettuccine made from 1/2 basic dough recipe (page 28) or 1 pound dried fettuccine

4 teaspoons chopped parsley

Basil to garnish

**Serves 4**

**4** Divide among 4 serving plates and sprinkle each with a teaspoon of chopped parsley; garnish with basil.

# Fettuccine all'Amatriciana
## Hot Fettuccine with Bacon

Some like it hot. For those who like it hotter, mince the chili pepper, seeds and all, before using. This pasta was named after the town of Amatriciana, in the Rome region, where the recipe originated.

In a large pot, bring 3 quarts of water to a boil with 3 tablespoons salt. Now prepare the sauce.

**Ingredients:**

10 ounces bacon

1 large ripe tomato

1/4 cup olive oil

6 large garlic cloves, each cut lengthwise into 4 slices

2 tablespoons chopped onion

1 chili pepper

1/2 cup dry white wine

2 cups Napoletana tomato sauce (page 40)

Salt to taste

Fettuccine made from 1/2 basic dough recipe (page 28) or 1 pound dried fettuccine

**Serves 4**

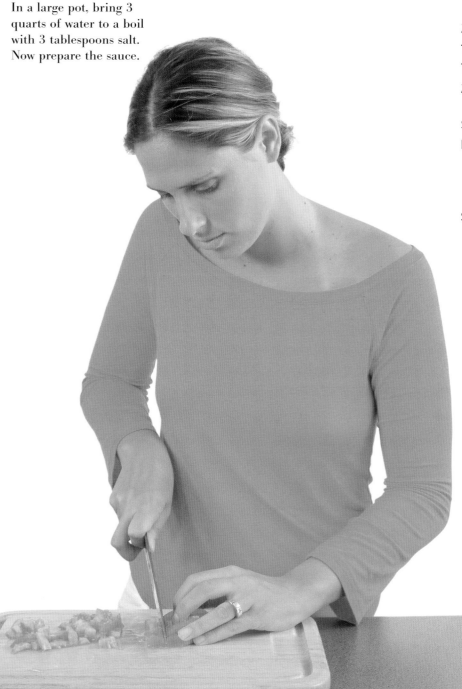

**1** Cut the bacon into 1/4" thick cubes, and the tomato into 1/4" cubes. Set aside.

**2** Heat the olive oil in a large skillet, and add the garlic. Sauté until just slightly golden.

**3** Add the onion, bacon and chili pepper. Sauté until the bacon is browned and crispy.

Add the tomato cubes and wine and let cook over low heat for 10 minutes, stirring occasionally.

Pour in the tomato sauce. Season with salt to taste.

Drop the fettuccine in the water and cook for 4 minutes for fresh pasta or according to package directions for dried pasta. Drain.

Mix the fettuccine with the sauce and stir to coat the noodles well.

Divide among 4 serving plates and serve immediately.

# Fettuccine agli Spinaci
## Fettuccine with Spinach

In a hurry? This is a quick sauce I like to make for friends. Sometimes, I use a handful of cherry tomatoes instead of a large tomato. And—although I don't—you can peel the tomato or cherry tomatoes if preferred.

In a large pot, bring 3 quarts of water to a boil with 3 tablespoons salt. Now prepare the sauce.

**Ingredients:**

1 pound fresh spinach

1/4 cup olive oil

5 large garlic cloves, each cut lengthwise into 4 slices

1 large ripe tomato, cut into 1/4" cubes

1/2 cup dry white wine

Fettuccine made from 1/2 basic dough recipe (page 28) or 1 pound dried fettuccine

Salt

Coarsely ground black pepper

4 heaping tablespoons freshly grated Parmesan cheese

**Serves 4**

1 Stem the spinach and rinse well to remove grit. Dry thoroughly and chop coarsely.

2 Heat the olive oil in a large skillet and add the garlic. Sauté until golden.

**3** Add the tomato and fresh spinach and cook, stirring, for 2 minutes.

**4** Add the wine.

**5** This is also the right time to drop the fettuccine in the water. Cook for 4 minutes for fresh pasta or according to package directions for dried pasta. Drain.

**6** Season the sauce with salt and pepper and add the pasta. Mix gently— just until the sauce evenly coats the noodles.

**7** Divide among serving plates and sprinkle grated Parmesan cheese on each serving.

# Fettuccine ai Broccoli
## Fettuccine with Broccoli

Fresh, lush green broccoli is one of my favorite vegetables, and it's healthy, too! Some people like to top this pasta dish with Parmesan cheese, but I feel it disguises the flavor of this marvelous vegetable.

**Ingredients:**

2 pounds fresh broccoli

1 large red bell pepper

1/4 cup olive oil

4 garlic cloves, each cut lengthwise into 4 slices

1 chili pepper

1 cup dry white wine

1/2 recipe fresh fettuccine or 1 pound dried fettuccine

Salt

Black pepper

**Serves 4**

*1* Cut the flowerets from the broccoli. Save the stems for another use.

*2* Cook the flowerets uncovered in boiling salted water for 7 minutes. Drain well.

*3* Drop the flowerets in a bowl of ice water to stop the cooking process, then drain.

*4* Grill the pepper on top of a gas burner or under the grill until black spots appear. Turn frequently.

**5** Remove with tongs and place in a paper bag. Leave it closed for 10 minutes (the steam loosens the skin), then peel off the skin and cut julienne-style.

**6** In a large pot, bring 3 quarts of water to a boil with 3 tablespoons salt.

**7** Heat the olive oil in a large skillet and sauté the garlic until golden. Add the chili pepper and sauté for 1 minute.

**8** Add the broccoli and pepper slices and stir until coated with oil, then pour in the white wine and reduce the liquid to half over high heat.

**9** Cook fettuccine 4 minutes for fresh pasta or according to package directions for dried pasta. Drain well and add to the skillet. Mix. Season with salt and pepper, divide into 4 portions and serve.

# My Fettuccine Primavera
## Vegetable Fettuccine

*Primavera* means "spring" in Italian, and there are as many variations on this dish as there are Italians. And while I know that in America, Fettuccine Primavera is usually made with a lot of vegetables, I prefer this simple one—it really reminds me of the red poppies and young greens carpeting the hillsides of Sardinia in spring.

**Ingredients:**

1/4 cup olive oil

5 garlic cloves, each cut lengthwise into 4 slices

1 chili pepper

7 ounces arugula

2 cups Napoletana tomato sauce (page 40)

2 cups cherry tomatoes (about 25), halved (or quartered if large)

1/2 recipe fresh fettuccine or 1 pound dried fettuccine

**Serves 4**

In a large pot, bring 3 quarts of water to a boil with 3 tablespoons salt.

Heat the oil in a large skillet over medium heat and sauté the garlic until golden. Add the chili pepper and sauté an additional minute.

Stir in the arugula leaves and cook until just wilted. Pour in the tomato sauce.

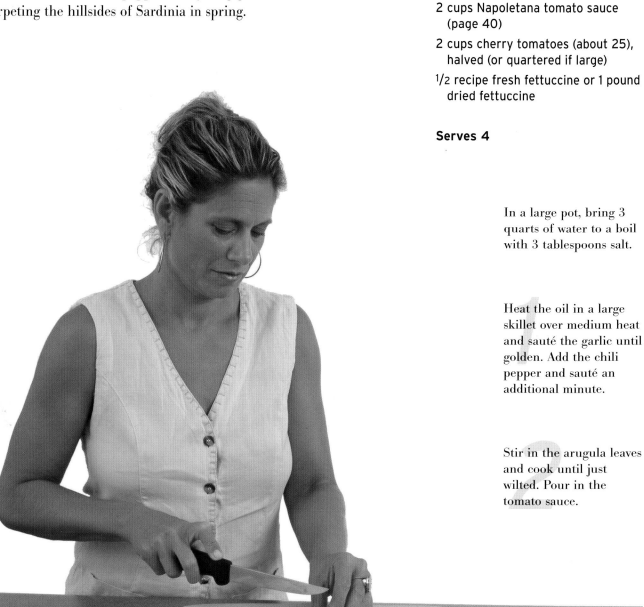

Add the tomatoes and let cook 5 minutes, stirring occasionally.

Cook fresh fettuccine for 4 minutes, or dried pasta according to package directions. Drain well and transfer to the skillet. Mix until just blended, and serve immediately.

**CARLO'S TIP:**
Always swirl the arugula leaves well in a bowl filled with several changes of water to remove grit, and save a few for garnish.

# Salsa di Noci
## Fettuccine with Walnut Sauce

The ancient Greeks pressed walnuts for oil even before the Romans (as early as the beginning of the fourth century BC), and in Roman folklore it was believed that the gods feasted on them. Considered healthy and symbolic of fertility, they were thrown by the bridegroom at Roman weddings, much as we throw rice at weddings today.

For this recipe, you'll need to toast the nuts in the oven at 350°F for 10 minutes, shaking the pan occasionally.

To make green fettuccine, use the recipe for Green (Spinach) Pasta Dough on page 34.

**Ingredients:**

3 1/2 ounces (1/2 cup) toasted walnut halves

1 clove garlic, minced

3 1/2 tablespoons olive oil

2 1/2 tablespoons freshly grated Parmesan cheese

Salt

Coarsely ground black pepper

1/2 recipe fresh green fettuccine or 1 pound dried green fettuccine

1/4 cup unsalted butter

**Serves 4**

1 In a large pot, bring 3 quarts of water to a boil with 3 tablespoons salt.

2 Put the toasted walnuts in a food processor and chop finely, using brief on-and-off pulses. (Do not grind to a powder.)

3 Place the garlic, olive oil, Parmesan, salt and pepper in a medium bowl.

4 Cook the fettuccine for 4 minutes for fresh pasta, or according to package directions for dried pasta. Drain.

Melt the butter in a large skillet over low heat. Add the walnuts and cook, stirring, about 3 minutes.

Place the drained fettuccine in a bowl, add both the walnut-butter and garlic-Parmesan mixtures, toss and serve.

# Fettuccine alla Siciliana
## Sicilian-Style Fettuccine

The first thing I do when I come into my restaurant in the morning is salt the eggplant slices and let them stand while I prepare the rest of the ingredients. That way, they are especially tender. Make sure to dry the eggplant slices before you fry them.

For this recipe, use a drier form of ricotta if possible.

**Ingredients:**

1 large eggplant (1 pound)

Coarse salt

Vegetable oil for frying

1/4 cup olive oil

4 garlic cloves, each cut lengthwise into 4 slices

1 chili pepper

2 cups Napoletana tomato sauce (page 40)

Fettuccine made from 1/2 basic dough recipe (page 28), or 1 pound dried fettuccine

6 ounces ricotta cheese

1 fresh basil for garnish

**Serves 4**

*1* Slice the eggplant crosswise into 1/2" slices.

*2* Place in a colander and sprinkle lightly with salt. Mix to lightly coat the slices.

*3* Cover with a kitchen towel and let stand at least 2 hours, until all the bitter juices have drained out. Rinse and pat dry.

*4* Heat 1 inch of oil in a large frying pan and sauté the eggplant on both sides until golden brown. Drain the slices on absorbent paper.

*5* In a large pot, bring 3 quarts of water to a boil with 3 tablespoons salt.

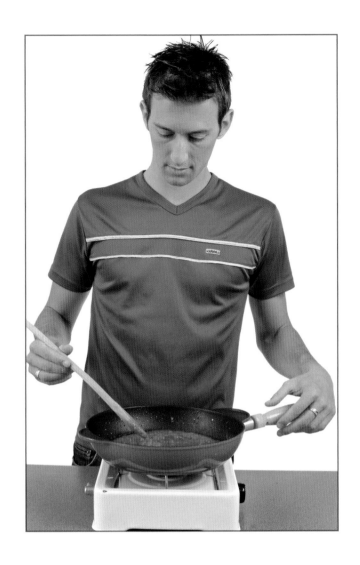

**6** Wash and dry the same frying pan in which you cooked the eggplant. Heat the olive oil and sauté the garlic until golden. Add the chili pepper and cook for 1 minute.

**7** Stir in the tomato sauce.

**8** Drop the fettuccine in the pot of water and cook for 4 minutes for fresh pasta or according to package directions for dried pasta. Drain.

**9** Transfer the fettuccine to the prepared sauce and mix to coat the strands.

**10** Divide the pasta among 4 serving plates. Top with about 5 overlapping eggplant slices. Crumble the ricotta cheese on top, and garnish with basil.

# Lasagne

# How to Make Fresh Lasagne Noodles

Everybody loves lasagne—one of the best-known Italian dishes to reach America. In Italy, it's the classic dish we eat on Sundays. (In fact, just thinking of lasagne makes me remember the taste of my mother's.) In our family, lasagne is a source of competition—because my two brothers and three sisters each think they make the best. (But the truth is that I do!)

In a cool climate, fresh, uncooked noodles can be kept, covered, at room temperature for an hour or two, but if it's warm outside or inside your house, they'll get too sticky if you leave them out. So if you're not going to use them immediately, freeze the uncooked noodles in layers, with wax paper between the layers. When ready to cook, remove the paper and drop the noodles straight into the boiling water. (No need to defrost.)

**Ingredients:**

1 pound durum semolina

3 medium eggs, at room temperature

1 tablespoon olive oil

**Serves 8**

1 Sift the flour into a bowl.

2 In a medium bowl, beat the eggs together briskly with a wire whisk or fork.

3 Put the semolina, beaten eggs and olive oil into the bowl of the food processor.

Beginning at medium speed, mix all the ingredients until the mixture forms a ball around the blade.

Remove from the food processor and place on a lightly floured work surface. Sprinkle a little flour on top.

Cover with a cloth towel and let rest for 10 minutes.

Divide the dough into 2 equal portions. Knead half of the dough at a time for a minute or two until no longer sticky, adding a little more flour if necessary.

Using a lightly floured rolling pin, shape one portion of dough into a 9" x 4" oblong, no more than $\frac{1}{2}$" thick.

Cover the oblong with a kitchen towel and repeat the process using the other half of the dough. Cover each oblong while working on the other.

Now shape the dough in the pasta machine, starting with the large roller. Position the machine on setting number 1 and use one hand to feed the dough between the rollers (while you crank the handle with the other hand), until it comes out the other side. (The dough will still be thick.)

**11** Change the number to 3 and feed the dough in again.

**12** Change the number to 5 (the thinnest setting), and feed the dough in slowly once more.

**13** Cut each oblong crosswise into 3 pieces. You will have 6 lasagne noodles. Keep covered until ready to cook.

**14** In a large pot, bring 3 quarts of water to a boil with 3 tablespoons salt. Add the 6 lasagne noodles and cook for 5 minutes.

**15** Carefully drain the noodles and rinse in cold water to stop the cooking process.

**16** Place the noodles on a tablecloth or kitchen towel and lay them flat.

Now you are ready to make any of the lasagne recipes in this chapter.

# Lasagne di Carne
## Meat Lasagne

I always use fresh lasagne noodles for making my lasagne—never the packaged ones and never, ever the ones that require no cooking (I think they taste like cardboard). If you want to use packaged noodles, follow the cooking directions on the package.

**Ingredients:**

6 fresh lasagne noodles (page 72) or half of a 1-pound package of dried lasagne noodles, cooked

2 1/2 cups Bolognese sauce (page 38)

4 cups Béchamel sauce (page 42)

3/4 cup freshly grated Parmesan cheese

**Serves 8**

Lay down 2 fresh pasta leaves, or enough cooked dried pasta leaves to cover the bottom of a 12" x 9" lasagne pan (or its equivalent).

Pour 1/2 of the Bolognese sauce over the leaves and use a spatula to spread it evenly.

Pour 1 1/4 cups Béchamel sauce over the Bolognese and spread this evenly as well.

**4** Sprinkle ¹/4 cup of grated Parmesan on top.

**5** Make another layer of 2 fresh pasta leaves, the remaining Bolognese sauce, 1¹/4 cups Béchamel and ¹/4 cup of Parmesan cheese.

**6** Top with the remaining pasta leaves, Béchamel, and Parmesan.

**7** Bake in a preheated 350°F oven for 25 minutes. Serve hot.

# Lasagne di Spinaci
## Spinach Lasagne

I always like to start with fresh spinach for this recipe, but for convenience sake you can also use frozen whole-leaf spinach, which I find superior to the chopped variety. (You will be chopping it more finely anyway, in the food processor.) For a lovely variation, use lasagne noodles made with Italian herb pasta (page 33).

**Ingredients:**

2 cups drained cooked fresh or frozen leaf spinach

8 tablespoons grated Parmesan cheese

4 tablespoons Emmental or Gruviera (Gruyère) cheese

1 pound 6 ounces Ricotta cheese

1 egg

4 cups Béchamel sauce (page 42)

Salt

Black pepper

Nutmeg

6 fresh lasagne noodles (page 72) or half of a 1-pound package of dried lasagne noodles, cooked

3 tablespoons breadcrumbs

**Serves 8**

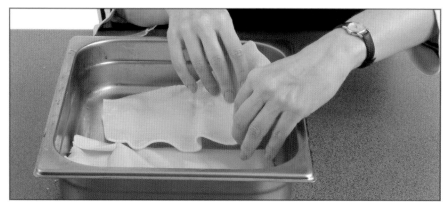

Put the spinach into a wire-mesh strainer and press to squeeze out as much moisture as possible. Transfer the spinach to a food processor and chop finely, almost to a paste.

In a small bowl, mix the Parmesan and Emmental or Gruviera cheeses together. In a separate bowl, mix the spinach, ricotta and egg.

Add 1 1/4 cups Béchamel sauce and 4 tablespoons of the Parmesan cheese mixture to the spinach-ricotta mixture. Season with salt, pepper and nutmeg.

Lay 2 fresh pasta leaves or enough cooked dried pasta leaves to cover the bottom of a 12" by 9" lasagne pan (or its equivalent).

Pour half of the spinach-ricotta mixture on top and use a spatula to spread it evenly.

Pour 1¹/4 cups Béchamel sauce on top, and sprinkle with 4 tablespoons of the Parmesan mixture. Make another layer of 2 fresh pasta leaves, the remaining spinach-ricotta mixture, 1¹/4 cups Béchamel and 3 more tablespoons of the Parmesan cheese mixture.

Top with the remaining pasta leaves, and the Béchamel and Parmesan mixture. Sprinkle with the breadcrumbs.

Bake in a preheated 350°F oven for 25 minutes. Serve hot.

# Lasagne di Salmone e Zucchine
## Lasagne with Salmon and Zucchini

This festive lasagne is perfect for special occasions.

**Ingredients:**

1 1/2 pounds fresh salmon

3 large zucchini (about 1 pound)

1/2 cup butter

2 medium onions (about 1 pound)

1 cup dry red wine

Salt

Black pepper

3 cups Béchamel sauce

6 fresh lasagne noodles (page 72) or half of a 1-pound package of lasagne noodles

4 tablespoons grated Parmesan mixed with 4 tablespoons grated Mozzarella

**Serves 8**

**3** Melt the butter in a skillet and add the onions. Cook until lightly golden.

**4** Add the zucchini and cook 5 minutes, stirring occasionally until tender.

**5** Pour in the wine and let cook until all the liquid evaporates. Season with salt and pepper.

**1** Chop the salmon in a food processor until it forms a paste and set aside.

**2** Rinse and cut zucchini julienne-style. Cut the onions down the middle and slice thinly.

**6** Lay down 2 fresh pasta leaves or enough cooked dried pasta leaves to cover the bottom of a 12" by 9" lasagne pan (or its equivalent).

**7** Place the salmon paste over the noodles, and use a spatula to make an even layer.

**8** Pour 1¹/4 cups Béchamel sauce on top, and sprinkle with 2¹/2 tablespoons of the Parmesan mixture. Add another layer of 2 fresh pasta leaves, a layer of the zucchini-onion mixture, an additional 1¹/4 cups of Béchamel, and 2¹/2 more tablespoons of the Parmesan cheese mixture.

**9** Top with the remaining pasta leaves, Béchamel and Parmesan mixture. Bake in a preheated 350°F oven for 25 minutes. Serve hot.

# Lasagne alle Melanzane
## Eggplant Lasagne

My friend Frank, who was raised in Cincinnati, tells me that even his Irish mother learned to make Lasagne alle Melanzane, or what Americans call Eggplant Parmesan. (We also call it Melanzane alla Parmigiana.) Unlike other types of lasagne, this one does not contain lasagne noodles, but the process of layering is similar to lasagne, which is why I include it in this chapter.

**Ingredients:**

3 large eggplants (just a little over 2 pounds)

4 tablespoons salt

Vegetable oil for frying

3/4 cup freshly grated Parmesan cheese

3/4 cup Mozzarella cheese

2 cups Napoletana tomato sauce (page 40)

**Serves 8**

1 Cut the eggplant lengthwise into 1/4" slices, sprinkle with salt and let stand for 1 hour in a colander.

2 Rinse the eggplant slices briefly and pat dry.

3 In a large skillet, sauté the eggplant slices in 2" of hot vegetable oil, turning them until browned on both sides. Remove with a metal spatula and place on a paper towel to absorb excess oil.

4 Mix together Mozzarella and Parmesan.

**5** In a 9" x 12" lasagne or baking pan, make a layer of eggplant. Top with $^{1}/_{3}$ of the Napoletana and $^{1}/_{3}$ of the cheese. Repeat three times for three layers.

**6** Bake in a preheated 350°F oven for 20 minutes. Serve hot.

# Ravioli

# How to Make Fresh Ravioli

**Ingredients:**

1 pound durum semolina

3 medium eggs, at room temperature

1 tablespoon olive oil

**Serves 4**

*1* Sift the flour into a bowl.

*2* In a medium bowl, beat the eggs together briskly with a wire whisk or fork.

*3* Put the semolina, beaten eggs and olive oil into the bowl of the food processor.

*4* Beginning at medium speed, mix all the ingredients until the mixture forms a ball around the blade.

*5* Remove from the processor and place on a lightly floured work surface. Sprinkle a little flour on top. Cover with a cloth towel and let rest for 10 minutes.

**6** Divide the dough into 3 equal portions. Knead 1/3 of the dough at a time for a minute or two, until no longer sticky, adding a little more flour if necessary.

**7** Using a lightly floured rolling pin, shape one portion of dough at a time into a 9" x 4" oblong, no more than 1/2" thick.

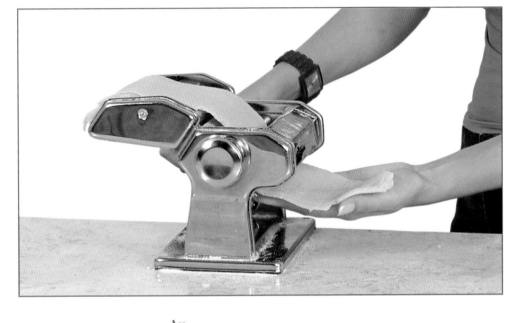

**8** Cover the oblong with a clean kitchen towel and repeat the process with the other two portions of the dough. Cover each oblong before working on the next.

**9** Now shape the dough in the pasta machine, starting with the large roller. Position the machine on setting number 1, and use one hand to feed the dough between the rollers (while you turn the crank with the other hand), until it comes out the other side. (The dough will still be thick.)

**10** Change the number to 3 and feed the dough in again.

**11** Change the number to 5 (the thinnest setting) and feed the dough in slowly once more.

**12** Place the special ravioli head on the pasta machine. Using the special pasta cutter (on small rollers) included with the machine, cut the dough leaves to fit the width of the ravioli head.

**13** Take one leaf at a time (keep the others covered), fold it in half, and feed the folded edge of it into the machine until it "catches."

**14** Drape the leaves one to each side, creating a space in which to put the stuffing.

**15** Place 2 heaping tablespoons of stuffing (see page 90) in the center.

*16* Turn the crank slowly until the finished ravioli comes through the other end. Repeat with the remaining leaves and stuffing.

Now you are ready to make any of the ravioli recipes in this chapter!

# Classic Ricotta Stuffing for Ravioli

If my restaurant clientele is any indication, it seems as if more and more people now prefer Ricotta-stuffed ravioli to meat-stuffed ones. When choosing Ricotta for ravioli stuffing, I recommend using a drier variety like Ricotta Romano.

This Ricotta stuffing will fill ravioli made with half a recipe of basic pasta dough (page 28), or one of my special pastas, like Italian herb pasta (page 33).

**Ingredients:**

1 pound fresh ricotta Romano

1 egg, lightly beaten

1/2 cup (slightly rounded) freshly grated Parmesan cheese

Salt

Ground black pepper

Nutmeg

**Serves 4**

1 In a medium bowl, mix Ricotta, egg and Parmesan cheese together using a wooden spoon. Add a pinch each of salt, pepper and nutmeg and blend well.

2 Cover the bowl and chill until ready to use. (This may be prepared several hours in advance.)

To stuff ravioli, follow the directions on page 88, and pick one of the following delicious sauces to accompany them, like Pesto, All'Arancia, Al Tartufo Bianco or Burro e Parmigiano.
*Bravissimo!*

# Ravioli Ricotta al Pesto
## Ricotta-Stuffed Ravioli with Pesto

This is the easiest pasta sauce yet! Sometimes we Italians just add a little olive oil to homemade pesto as a sauce for ravioli. But mixing in a little cream is *fantastico*. Try it—and you'll see what I mean.

**Ingredients:**

1 cup sweet cream

4 tablespoons pesto (page 43)

Ricotta-stuffed ravioli made from half of the basic pasta dough recipe (page 28), or 1 1/2 pounds prepared Ricotta-stuffed ravioli

**Serves 4**

*1* In a large pot, bring 3 quarts of water to a boil with 3 tablespoons salt.

*2* Pour the cream into a saucepan and cook on medium-high heat until reduced to 1/2 cup. Remove from heat and blend in the pesto.

*3* Cook fresh ravioli 7 minutes or packaged ravioli according to package directions. Drain and transfer to a bowl. Mix in the pesto sauce and serve immediately.

# Ravioli Ricotta all'Arancia

Ricotta-Stuffed Ravioli with Orange Sauce

**Ingredients:**

1 large orange

2 heaping tablespoons butter

1 large onion (1/2 pound), finely minced

4 tablespoons brandy

1 cup sweet cream

Salt

Freshly ground black pepper

Nutmeg

Ricotta-stuffed ravioli made from half of the basic pasta dough recipe (page 28), or 1 1/2 pounds prepared Ricotta-stuffed ravioli

**Serves 4**

1 In a large pot, bring 3 quarts of water to a boil with 3 tablespoons salt.

2 Rinse the orange and use a zester to remove the rind in thin strips.

3 Juice half of the orange and set it aside.

4 In a large skillet, melt the butter over low heat. Add the onion and half of the orange rind. Cook on medium heat, stirring often, until golden.

5 Add the orange juice and reduce by half.

**6** Pour in the brandy, tip the frying pan and let it ignite from the fire. (If using an electric burner, you'll have to ignite the brandy carefully with a match.) Let the fire burn out.

**7** When the fire is extinguished, add the cream and continue cooking on medium heat until reduced by half. Season with a pinch each of salt, pepper and nutmeg.

**8** Cook fresh ravioli 7 minutes or packaged ravioli according to package directions. Drain well and transfer to a bowl.

**9** Pour on the sauce and serve garnished with the remaining orange rind.

# Ravioli Ricotta al Tartufo Bianco

Ricotta-Stuffed Ravioli with White Truffle Sauce

This is considered a gourmet sauce in Italy, and it is served especially from October to December, when *tartufi* (truffles) grow in northeastern Italy. It is well known that the best white truffles come from Alba, south of Turin. Since they are relatively rare, they are very expensive, but anyone who tastes them will agree that their flavor and unique scent are incomparable. You'll need both tartufo paste and a small white truffle for this recipe.

**Ingredients:**

Ricotta-stuffed ravioli made from half of the basic pasta dough recipe (page 28), or 1 1/2 pounds prepared Ricotta-stuffed ravioli

3 tablespoons butter

Salt

Ground white pepper

2 tablespoons truffle paste

1 small white truffle

**Serves 4**

1 In a large pot, bring 3 quarts of water to a boil with 3 tablespoons salt. Cook fresh ravioli 7 minutes or packaged ravioli according to package directions.

2 While the pasta is cooking, hold a large skillet over the pasta pot and melt the butter, salt and white pepper together.

3 Blend in the truffle paste.

4 Drain the ravioli, place in the butter mixture and mix to coat the ravioli with the sauce. Grate the white truffle on top and serve.

# Ravioli Ricotta al Burro e Parmigiano

## Ricotta-Stuffed Ravioli with Butter and Parmesan Cheese

This is the Italian version of the Alfredo sauce that my friend Frank tells me is so popular in America—and which most Italians aren't familiar with. In fact, the first time a customer ordered it in our family restaurant, I had to ask my brother to look up the recipe! In the classic Alfredo, the cheese is melted in slightly reduced cream, but since Italians don't like to use a lot of cream, our closest version is this butter and black pepper sauce. For best results, use only freshly ground black pepper.

**Ingredients:**

Ricotta-stuffed ravioli made from half of the basic pasta dough recipe (page 28), or 1 1/2 pounds prepared Ricotta-stuffed ravioli

2 1/2 tablespoons butter

Salt

Freshly ground black pepper

1/2 cup freshly grated Parmesan cheese

**Serves 4**

*1* In a large pot, bring 3 quarts of water to a boil with 3 tablespoons salt. Cook fresh ravioli 7 minutes or packaged ravioli according to package directions.

*2* While the pasta is cooking, melt the butter slowly in a small frying pan over low heat and add a good pinch of salt.

*3* Drain the pasta, transfer to a bowl and add the melted butter.

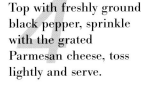

*4* Top with freshly ground black pepper, sprinkle with the grated Parmesan cheese, toss lightly and serve.

# Classic Spinach Stuffing for Ravioli

For all the spinach recipes I've given you, I always start with fresh spinach. I rinse the leaves well, remove the stems, and drop the leaves in a pot with a pinch of salt. Then I cover the pot with a tight-fitting lid and, using only the water left clinging to the leaves, cook the leaves on medium-low heat until they wilt. Always drain spinach as thoroughly as possible before using. If you prefer, you may use frozen leaf spinach for this recipe instead.

**Ingredients:**

2 cups cooked and drained fresh or frozen spinach

10 1/2 ounces Ricotta cheese, preferably Ricotta Romano

1 egg

1/2 cup freshly grated Parmesan cheese

Ground black pepper

Salt

Nutmeg

**Serves 4**

**1** Put the spinach in a colander, and press down with the palm of your hand to remove any excess moisture.

**2** Finely chop the spinach in a food processor.

**3** Mix the Ricotta, egg and Parmesan cheese in a small bowl, using a wooden spoon. Blend well.

**4** Add the chopped spinach and season with a good pinch each of salt and pepper, and a dash of nutmeg.

To stuff ravioli, follow the directions on page 88, and pick one of the following delicious sauces to go with them: Burro e Salvia, Al Timo in Salsa Rosa, or Panna e Funghi.

# Ravioli Spinaci Burro e Salvia

## Spinach-Stuffed Ravioli with Butter and Sage Sauce

This easy dish, enhanced by the aroma and taste of pungent fresh sage, is a classic of the Italian kitchen. (For the amazing properties of sage, see page 25.) This sauce is also great with Ricotta-stuffed or shrimp-stuffed ravioli.

**Ingredients:**

Spinach-stuffed ravioli made from half of the basic pasta dough recipe (page 28), or 1 1/2 pounds prepared spinach-stuffed ravioli

2 tablespoons butter

8–9 fresh sage leaves

Freshly ground black pepper

Parmesan cheese

**Serves 4**

2 While the ravioli is cooking, melt the butter in a large skillet on the lowest possible heat and add the sage leaves. Cook 1 minute, stirring gently. Remove the pan from the heat.

3 Drain the ravioli, return the skillet with the melted butter and sage leaves to the heat, and add the ravioli. Mix gently to coat the ravioli with the sauce. Sprinkle the top with freshly ground black pepper and Parmesan cheese, and serve.

1 In a large pot, bring 3 quarts of water to a boil with 3 tablespoons salt. Cook fresh ravioli 7 minutes or packaged ravioli according to package directions.

# Ravioli Spinaci al Timo in Salsa Rosa

## Spinach-Stuffed Ravioli with Thyme and Pink Sauce

**1** In a large pot, bring 3 quarts of water to a boil with 3 tablespoons salt. Cook fresh ravioli 7 minutes or packaged ravioli according to package directions. While the ravioli is cooking, make the sauce.

**2** Melt the butter in a large skillet. Add the thyme and cook for 1 minute, stirring occasionally.

**Ingredients:**

Spinach-stuffed ravioli made from half of the green spinach pasta dough recipe (page 34), or 1½ pounds prepared spinach-stuffed ravioli

2 ½ tablespoons butter

1 teaspoon fresh thyme leaves, chopped

4 tablespoons vodka

1 cup sweet cream

2 tablespoons Napoletana tomato sauce (page 40)

Salt

Freshly ground black pepper

Nutmeg

**Serves 4**

**3** Add the vodka and tip the pan until it catches fire. (If using an electric burner, you'll have to ignite the vodka carefully with a match.) Let the fire burn out.

**4** When the fire is extinguished, add the cream, and reduce the liquids by one-third.

**5** Stir in the tomato sauce and reduce by another third. Season with a little salt, pepper, and nutmeg.

**6** Drain the ravioli well and place in the skillet. Stir to coat the ravioli with the sauce and serve.

# Ravioli Spinaci Panna e Funghi
## Spinach-Stuffed Ravioli with Cream and Mushroom Sauce

**Ingredients:**

Spinach-stuffed ravioli made from half of the green spinach pasta dough recipe (page 34), or 1 1/2 pounds prepared spinach-stuffed ravioli

2 tablespoons butter

4 large garlic cloves, each cut lengthwise into 4 slices

1 1/2 cups coarsely chopped fresh mushrooms

1/2 cup dry red wine

1 cup sweet cream

Salt

Ground black pepper

Chives to garnish

**Serves 4**

1. In a large pot, bring 3 quarts of water to a boil with 3 tablespoons salt. Cook fresh ravioli 7 minutes or packaged ravioli according to package directions. While the ravioli is cooking, make the sauce.

2. Meanwhile, melt the butter in a large skillet and sauté the garlic over medium heat until golden.

3. Add the mushrooms and let cook until the mushrooms wilt and the volume is reduced by half.

**4** Pour in the red wine and cook over medium heat until the liquid is reduced by half.

**5** Add the cream, cook over medium heat until reduced by half, and season with salt and pepper.

**6** Drain the pasta and place in a serving bowl. Pour on the sauce and toss gently to mix.

**7** Garnish with chives (or chopped fresh oregano, if you like).

# Shrimp Stuffing for Ravioli

Whether served as an appetizer or a main course, these very special shrimp-stuffed ravioli add a gourmet touch to any meal. Use only fresh shrimp for this recipe—frozen shrimp contain too much water and will be rubbery.

**Ingredients:**

1 pound medium-sized fresh shrimp

1/2 cup bread crumbs

1 medium egg

2 tablespoons fresh oregano, chopped

Salt

Ground black pepper

**Serves 4**

*1* Rinse, peel and use the tip of a sharp knife to de-vein the shrimps.

*2* Chop in a food processor to form a paste.

*3* Add bread crumbs, egg and oregano and process briefly.

*4* Season to taste with salt and pepper. If not using immediately, transfer to a plastic container, cover and store in the refrigerator for up to 3–4 hours.

To stuff ravioli, follow the directions on page 88. Serve them with festive Frutti di Mare, Brandy Sauce, or Vodka Sauce.

# Ravioli ai Gamberi con Frutti di Mare

## Shrimp-Stuffed Ravioli with Seafood Sauce

**Ingredients:**

12 large mussels

1 1/2 ounces calamari (squid)

12 large shrimp

1 1/2 ounces chopped octopus
  tentacles

2 tablespoons olive oil

4 garlic cloves, each sliced
  lengthwise into 4 pieces

1/2–1 chili pepper

1/2 cup dry red wine

1 cup Napoletana sauce (page 40)

Salt

Shrimp-stuffed ravioli made from
  half of the basic pasta
  dough recipe (page 28), or 1 1/2
  pounds prepared shrimp-
  stuffed ravioli

4 teaspoons chopped parsley

**Serves 4**

*1* Put the mussels in a bowl of cold water. Use a paring knife to cut away the beards protruding from the shell of each mussel. Scrub the mussels with a stiff brush to remove all the grime. Repeat 3 times, each time with a fresh change of cold water.

*2* Rinse the calamari well, and remove any grit on the inside. Slice into 1" rings.

*3* Peel and de-vein the shrimp, but leave the tails on.

*4* Rinse the octopus well, and remove the mouth at the bottom. Chop into 1/2" pieces.

In a large pot, bring 3 quarts of water to a boil with 3 tablespoons salt. Now prepare the sauce.

Heat the olive oil in the skillet and add the garlic and chili pepper. Cook until golden, stirring constantly.

Add the mussels, calamari, octopus, and shrimp; cover and sauté over high heat for 1 minute. Remove the seafood from the skillet and set aside.

**8** Add the wine and cook over high heat until reduced by half. Add the tomato sauce. Cook for 1 minute and remove from heat.

**9** Drop the ravioli into the pot of boiling water, cook for 7 minutes or according to package directions, and drain.

**10** Return the seafood to the sauce and warm again for 1 minute. Season with salt, add the ravioli to the sauce and mix to coat. Serve garnished with chopped parsley on top.

# Ravioli ai Gamberi al Brandy

## Shrimp-Stuffed Ravioli with Brandy Sauce

Looking for something simple yet spectacular? Your friends will think you're a wonder with this one!

**Ingredients:**

12 large shrimp

3 tablespoons butter

4 tablespoons brandy

1 cup sweet cream

2 tablespoons Napoletana sauce (page 40)

Shrimp-stuffed ravioli made from half of the basic pasta dough recipe (page 28), or 1¹/₂ pounds prepared shrimp-stuffed ravioli

Salt

Ground black pepper

1 rounded tablespoon thinly sliced fresh mint

**Serves 4**

**1** In a large pot, bring 3 quarts of water to a boil with 3 tablespoons salt.

**2** Peel the shrimp and cut into ¹/₄" pieces.

**3** Melt the butter in a large skillet over medium heat and quickly sauté the shrimp, stirring constantly, until they just change color. Remove the shrimp from the pan and set aside.

**4** Increase heat to high, and add half the brandy. Tip the pan to ignite the brandy. (If using an electric burner, you'll have to ignite the brandy carefully with a match.) Wait until the fire goes out.

**5** Blend in the cream and tomato sauce, and let cook over medium heat until reduced by half. Season with salt and pepper and set aside.

**6** Cook fresh shrimp-stuffed ravioli for 7 minutes, or packaged ravioli according to package directions.

**7** One minute before the pasta is ready, reheat the sauce over low heat. Add the shrimp and remaining brandy, and mix over medium heat for a minute or two until heated through.

**8** Garnish with fresh mint and serve.

# Ravioli ai Gamberi alla Vodka

## Shrimp-Stuffed Ravioli with Vodka Sauce

**Ingredients:**

3 tablespoons butter

1/3 cup finely chopped onion

12 medium shrimp, peeled and cut in 1/4" pieces

6 tablespoons vodka

1 cup sweet cream

Salt

Freshly ground black pepper

Shrimp-stuffed ravioli made from half of the basic pasta dough recipe (page 28), or 1 1/2 pounds prepared shrimp-stuffed ravioli

4 teaspoons snipped chives

**Serves 4**

1 In a large pot, bring 3 quarts of water to a boil with 3 tablespoons salt.

2 Melt the butter in a large skillet. Add the onion and cook over medium-low heat until golden, stirring occasionally.

3 Add the shrimp pieces and sauté on medium heat just until they change color. Remove the shrimp from the pan.

**4** Add half of the vodka to the skillet and tip the pan to ignite it. (If using an electric burner, you'll have to ignite the vodka carefully with a match.) Let the fire go out.

**5** Add the cream and reduce by half. Season with salt and pepper. Remove from heat and set aside.

**6** Cook fresh shrimp-stuffed ravioli for 7 minutes or packaged ravioli according to package directions. Drain well.

**7** One minute before the pasta is ready, reheat the sauce over low heat, add the shrimp and remaining vodka, and mix over medium heat for a minute or two until heated through.

**8** Garnish with fresh chives and serve.

# How to Make Fresh Tortellini

Tortellini might be called an all-purpose form of ravioli, because in addition to eating them in sauce, we like to serve them in soup. Tortellini originated in the area around Bologna, where they are traditionally served on Christmas. Unlike ravioli, they are always stuffed with meat. They are called *Tortellini di Carne* in Italian.

Although the process is somewhat time-consuming, tortellini can be prepared in advance and frozen in one layer. Do not defrost before cooking—the cooking time will be the same as indicated in the recipe. Tortellini taste great with Napoletana sauce (page 40) or Panna e Funghi (page 100).

*1* Prepare the leaves of pasta as described in the basic pasta dough recipe (page 28). Cut into 4" squares.

*2* Indent the center of a square with your finger.

*3* Place a 1" ball of filling in the indent.

**Fold over one corner of the square to form a triangle. Pinch the edges to seal.**

**Press the opposite corners of the triangle together and pinch to seal. The tortellini will look like little priests' hats. Repeat with the remaining triangles.**

To cook, heat a large pot with 3 quarts water and 3 tablespoons salt. Cook for 8 minutes and drain. Serve with the desired sauce.

# Meat Stuffing for Tortellini

**Ingredients:**

4 tablespoons olive oil

1/4 cup minced onion

1/3 cup minced carrot

2 large garlic cloves, minced, pressed or chopped

10 ounces lean ground beef

3 1/2 ounces ground turkey

1/2 cup dry red wine

1/4 cup freshly grated Parmesan cheese

1 tablespoon minced parsley

Salt

Ground black pepper

Bread crumbs

Fresh tortellini made from half of the basic pasta dough (page 28)

**Serves 4-5**

1 Heat the olive oil in a large skillet, and sauté the onions, carrots and garlic for five minutes, stirring often.

2 Add the turkey and beef, and cook over medium-high heat, stirring constantly, until well done.

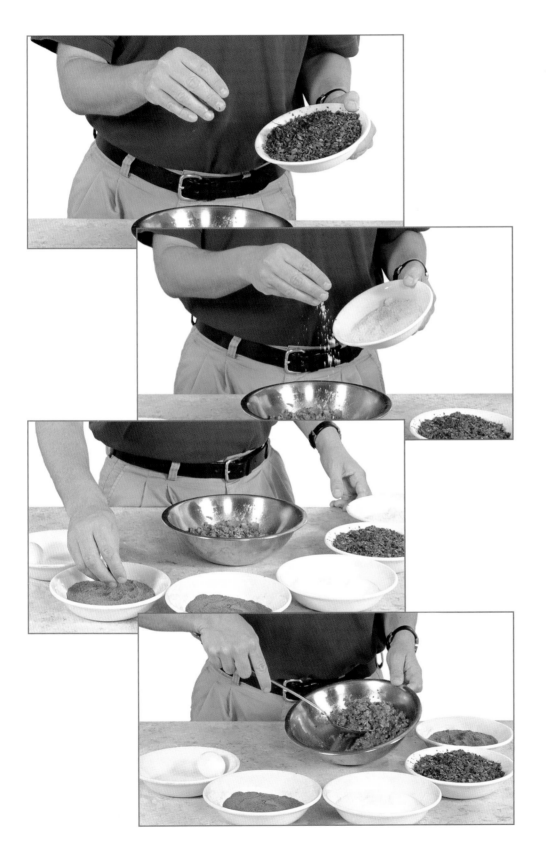

Add the red wine. Reduce until the wine is fully absorbed and the mixture is dry. Remove from heat and set aside to cool.

Add the Parmesan, parsley, salt and pepper and mix well with a wooden spoon.

Using your hands, shape the mixture into a ball, adding bread crumbs as necessary so the mixture holds together.

Prepare and stuff the tortellini according to the directions on page 110.

In a large pot, bring 3 quarts of water to a boil with 3 tablespoons salt. Drop the tortellini in and cook for 8 minutes. Drain and serve with the desired sauce.

# Tortellini Panna e Funghi
## Tortellini with Cream and Mushroom Sauce

**Ingredients:**

Tortellini made from half of a basic pasta dough recipe (page 28), or 1 1/2 pounds prepared tortellini

2 tablespoons butter

4 large garlic cloves, each cut lengthwise into 4 slices

1 1/2 cups coarsely chopped fresh mushrooms

1/2 cup dry red wine

1 cup sweet cream

Salt

Ground black pepper

4 teaspoons chopped parsley

**Serves 4**

**1** To cook, heat a large pot with 3 quarts water and 3 tablespoons salt. Cook for 8 minutes and drain. While the tortellini is cooking, make the sauce.

**2** Meanwhile, melt the butter in a large skillet and sauté the garlic over medium heat until golden.

**3** Add the mushrooms and let cook until the mushrooms wilt and the volume is reduced by half.

Pour in the red wine and cook over medium heat until the liquid is reduced by half.

Add the cream, cook over medium heat until reduced by half, and season with salt and pepper.

Drain the pasta and place in a serving bowl. Pour on the sauce and toss gently to mix.

Garnish with fresh parsley (or chopped fresh oregano, if you like).

# Gnocchi

# How to Make Fresh Gnocchi

When most people think of gnocchi, they think of potato gnocchi, which are indeed the most popular. But as you'll see on page 124, the Romans invented Gnocchi alla Romana, a delicious variation made with semolina.

Potato gnocchi actually originated in Verona, the city of love and the backdrop for the famous story of Romeo and Juliet. (Personally I'm not crazy about the place, because my soccer team lost to Verona once too often.)

For best results, cook the potatoes the day before because they have to be dry. I recommend using a ricer for the potatoes, in order to get the right consistency. Gnocchi can also be frozen in one layer for up to two days.

**Ingredients:**

2 pounds potatoes, rinsed and scrubbed but not peeled

1 1/4 cups flour

2 eggs, lightly beaten

3 pinches of salt

1/3 cup freshly grated Parmesan cheese

Extra flour

**Serves 4**

*1* Place potatoes in a large pot with enough cold water to cover them, and bring to a boil. Cook until fork-tender. (Small potatoes will take about 30 minutes, larger potatoes, longer.)

*2* Let the potatoes cool, peel them and put them through a ricer.

*3* Transfer to a bowl and use your hands to mix in the flour, eggs, salt and Parmesan cheese, until a compact ball is formed. It will be slightly sticky. If it's too wet, add more flour, a little at a time.

Lightly flour your hands. Roll out approximately 1/6 of the dough and shape it on a lightly floured board to make a cylinder 1/2" in diameter.

With a knife, cut the cylinder into 1" pieces. Sprinkle with a little flour and set aside. Repeat with the rest of the dough.

In a large pot, bring 3 quarts of water to a boil with 3 tablespoons salt. Add half the gnocchi and cook just until it floats, about 3 minutes. Drain and mix with the desired sauce. Serve immediately.

# Gnocchi ai Quattro Formaggi

## Gnocchi with Four Cheeses

In a large pot, bring 3 quarts of water to a boil with 3 tablespoons salt. Now make the sauce.

**1** Pour the cream into a saucepan and add the Gruyère cheese.

**2** Add the Fontina, Pecorino and Gorgonzola, stirring often over low heat until the cheeses are melted. Season with salt and pepper. Remove from heat.

**3** Drop the gnocchi into the water and cook 3 minutes. Reheat the sauce on low heat, drain the gnocchi and add to the sauce. Toss lightly to coat the gnocchi.

**Ingredients:**

1 1/2 cups sweet cream

3 tablespoons Gruviera (Gruyère) cheese

3 tablespoons Fontina cheese

2 tablespoons Pecorino Romano cheese

2 tablespoons Gorgonzola cheese

Salt

Black pepper to taste

Potato Gnocchi (page 118)

4 teaspoons parsley

**Serves 4**

**4** Garnish with parsley and serve.

# Gnocchi al Gorgonzola

## Gnocchi with Gorgonzola Sauce

This sauce originates in the area between my hometown of Milan and Turin, where they make the best Gorgonzola in Italy. In Italy we consider it a winter sauce, richly satisfying and warming especially in cold weather. There are two basic kinds of Gorgonzola available—one creamy and almost sweet, and the other piquant. Use the creamy kind for this recipe.

**Ingredients:**

1 1/2 cups sweet cream

5 ounces Gorgonzola cheese (1/2 cup crumbled)

Salt

Ground black pepper to taste

Potato Gnocchi (page 118)

1 tablespoon finely chopped toasted walnuts

**Serves 4**

**2** Drop the gnocchi into the water and cook 3 minutes. Reheat the sauce on low heat, drain the gnocchi, and add to the sauce. Toss lightly to coat.

**1** In a large pot, bring 3 quarts of water to a boil with 3 tablespoons salt. Now make the sauce.

**3** Garnish with the walnuts and serve.

**1** Place the cream and Gorgonzola in a saucepan and heat over low heat, stirring often, until the cheese is melted. Season with salt and pepper to taste. Set aside while preparing the gnocchi.

**CARLO'S TIP:**
**This sauce is also great on spaghettini.**

# Gnocchi con Funghi Porcini
## Gnocchi with Porcini Mushroom Sauce

Autumn—from September to November—is fresh porcini season in northern Italy, the time we used to go the mountains to collect these marvelous mushrooms. When we got home, my mother and I would sit in the kitchen and peel them one by one.

**Ingredients:**

10 1/2 ounces fresh porcini mushrooms, or 3 cups dried

3 tablespoons olive oil

3 medium cloves garlic, each cut lengthwise into 4 slices

3/4 cup dry white wine

Salt

Freshly ground black pepper

Potato Gnocchi (page 118)

4 teaspoons thyme

**Serves 4**

1 Wipe the fresh porcini mushrooms with a paper towel and peel using a small sharp knife. Slice lengthwise. (If using dried porcini, soak in warm water for 10–20 minutes until plumped.) Rinse well in several changes of water to remove any grit. Drain.

2 In a large pot, bring 3 quarts of water to a boil with 3 tablespoons salt. Now make the sauce.

3 Heat the olive oil in a large skillet and add the garlic. Sauté quickly over medium heat, stirring often until golden.

4 Add the fresh porcini and sauté over medium heat for 3–4 minutes, stirring occasionally until tender and just wilted (or sauté drained dry porcini 1 minute).

**5** Add the white wine to the sauce and cook over medium heat until reduced by half. Season with salt and pepper.

**6** While the sauce is cooking, drop the gnocchi into the water and cook 3 minutes.

**7** Drain the gnocchi and add to the sauce. Toss lightly to coat. Serve immediately, garnished with thyme.

# Gnocchi alla Romana

## Semolina Gnocchi

Potato gnocchi originated in northeastern Italy, where the potato was first introduced centuries ago. The Romans, however, developed their own version made out of semolina (a particular grind of wheat). They're both so good that I still can't decide which I like best!

**Ingredients:**

4 cups milk

Salt

Ground black pepper

Nutmeg

1 1/2 cups semolina (not durum semolina)

1/2 cup + 1 tablespoon butter

2 egg yolks

1/2 cup (slightly rounded) freshly grated Parmesan cheese

**Serves 4**

**1** Bring the milk to a boil in a large 2- to 3-quart pot over medium heat, and pour in the semolina gradually, stirring constantly with a wooden spoon to avoid lumps.

**2** Add a good pinch each of salt, pepper and nutmeg. Continue cooking and stirring on medium-low heat for about 3–4 minutes until the spoon can stand up straight in the center of the pot unsupported.

**3** Remove the pot from the heat and stir in 1/2 cup of the butter, the egg yolks and half of the Parmesan cheese. Mix well and set aside until cool enough to handle.

**4** Butter a baking sheet and spread the semolina a little less than 1/2" thick with a pastry knife. Let cool completely until the semolina is firm. (This can be prepared several hours ahead, then covered with plastic wrap and refrigerated.)

Using a 2" round pastry cutter or glass (dipped in hot water), cut circles out of the mixture. Gather up the remaining semolina, roll out again and cut out more circles until the mixture is used up.

Transfer the circles to a buttered baking dish and arrange them in a circular pattern from the outside in, with edges overlapping.

Sprinkle with the remaining Parmesan cheese, melt the remaining butter and distribute equally over the top, and bake in a preheated 350°F oven for 15 minutes or until golden brown. Serve hot.

# Index